Finding

My

Rhythm

By Alejandra Betancourt

Printed in the United States of America

ISBN-13: 978-0-578-47515-8

First Printed, 2019

Alejandra Betancourt

Alejandra.Betancourt1217@gmail.com

Cover Design by, A. Betancourt

This one is for me.

Finding My Rhythm

One can find inspiration from just about anywhere and anyone. I have so many amazing people surrounding me in my universe, I will never run out of emotions.

With that being said, I would like to thank as well as acknowledge

Edward, Madison, Michael, Paula (Lo-La), Marilyn, Johanna Marie, Monica, Vanessa, Amber, Gianna, Amelia, Jenni (Sassy), Leticia & my beautiful mother Elba

For the inspiration, I see and feel for each and every one of you.

I would also like to thank my 3 brightest stars again, Edward, Madison & Michael, because of you guys I can always find my way out of the darkness.

CONTENTS

1. Oh Father

I go to bed each night

With him by my side

With our fussing & our fighting

He's still my ride or die

I wake up every morning

With his chainsaw snoring

My kids, healthy & strong

Feisty but still growing

My body is not the same

I walk in constant pain

My face with many miles

But the grin always remains

We really don't have much

Our wallets on a diet

With the loudness all around
Our house, we live in silence

I'm blessed with all our blessings
I guess we're always guessing
It just cannot get better
Stress less with all our stressing

My Lord, Oh Father dear
I thank you for our have nots
For the little we do have
For the riches of our have gots

2. Forgive Me Not

Forgive me not
It's all my fault
Too many secrets
In my secret vault

Too many skeletons
In my walk in closet
Too many checks
Not enough deposits

Honesty
Was not priority
Pity me
I am no one's charity

Speak too much
Words unspoken

Right hand high

Promises broken

From my past

I have no shame

Financial gain

Pictures in frames

All is good

I am great

Forgive me not

For my mistakes

3. Dear Daughter

The world can be cold

This world can be cruel

Be your best friend

And follow your rules

Love yourself most

Put yourself first

The rest will then follow

Remember, things can be worse

You get what you give

So give it your all

When things come crumbling

You stay and stand tall

Words can hurt feelings

Try to be kind

Disrespect is not an option

Always speak your mind

Peace is important

Use prayer, it works

Believe in the power

You'll benefit the perks

Dear daughter

Be the best you

Believe in yourself

The way that I do

4. Lid

We said "I do"

And so we did

I found the container

To my lid

A perfect fit

We found in us

To love & honor

Forever trust

My apple pie

My sweet escape

My super hero

With many shapes

Above all others

My manly man

Love at 1st sight

Is where it began

It's not all great

We have our phases

Disagreements

Silent changes

There's no quitting

We do not play

This isn't a game

We do not stray

No giving up

We said "I do"

To our promises

We must be true

Love is hard

We are not perfect

When it's all said & done

Love is worth it

5. Savage Sisters

Savage sisters

Winter feast

Jealousy

Kills the beast

Who has more?

Who's the best?

Pass or fail

Theater test

Drama dancers

No wrong moves

Tap the loudest

Brightest shoes

Somber siblings

Fake the funk

Biggest gift

Smells like skunk

She said, he said

Story tellers

Cobweb tales

From the cellar

Mother's Day

Both so lonely

Too much pride

Both so phony

6. Butterflies in My Sky

A million memories fluttering in my mind

Like a million butterflies flying in the sky

With no direction, no rhythm or rhyme

Random thoughts can't capture one time

I remember the 1st time I saw that smile

In a folder marked fragile, in one of my files

With that 1 deep dimple, on your chin it lies

I put it away in this memory of mine

I remember your cries when 1st we met

How it stopped when you were placed on
my chest

How time stood still when you looked at me

And I store it all in my memories

The special treatment you gave to me

When I was younger and feeling sickly

And once in a while, in secrecy

Amongst my sibling you would favor me

So many butterflies fluttering at one time

A million miles a minute in my rapid mind

They can't be replaced nor be denied

They are all my butterflies in my sky

7. Déjà vu

Let's review the story

Why I don't change

Rearrange my person

While you remain the same

Look at you

Before pointing the finger

A man who sings

Who is not a singer

A man who changes

His ways for no one

Repeating mistakes

Whose life's a rerun

Who does not work

Yet, overpaid

With many faces

Masquerade

A revolving door

Going in circles

Lost in direction

Full of obstacles

Up-and-down

Side-to-side

I'm in pain

But never mind

You are hot

Fuming with fire

From the hurt

YOU are tired

A revolving door

Déjà vu

Look at me

NO! Look at you!

8. Born To Burn

I was born to burn

Because I'm on fire

I may get exhausted

But I never get tired

Mama ain't raise no fool

And she didn't raise a quitter

Sometimes things get shitty

And other days they get shittier

I always keep it moving

You can't stop my fight

You can't dent my day

And you can't dim my light

I am more than you

What I allow you to see

You worry about you

I will worry about me

I have my plan in action

I make many moves

Everything in my time

I have nothing to prove

I was born to burn

Because I am just so hot

You can't knock me down

I am who you are not

9. Those Where the Days

To each their own

Different Strokes

Like Mr. Drummond

I love all folks

Live & let live

Judgement free

Stay out my business

Let me breathe

Like The Fonz

Happy Days

Free to be me

In every way

Like Dwayne

Hey! Hey! Hey!

What's Happening!!

Those were the days

Remember Good Times?

What went wrong?

Damn! Damn! Damn!

Daddy's gone

So sensitive

Nothing is right

Live & let live

Like DY-NO-MITE!

10. Fuck You!

Fuck me!? NO! Fuck you!
For thinking I was fun
For making me laugh loud
For making me "The One"

For everyday you've taken
For those you took away
For painting me a picture
On a silver platter tray

For the introduction
That's taken me this far
For promising the world
And showing me the stars

For every word you spoke
For taking them all back

For making me the meal

And everyone a snack

For making me feel less

When I know I'm so much more

For all the disrespect

You shook me to the core

For such a waste of time

I wish I could redo

A lesson was well learned

Fuck Me!? NO! Fuck you!

11. Failures in Frames

I don't mean to complain

But I'm going to complain

About the weather outside

About the sun and the rain

About the past and the now

How things aren't the same

How everything has changed

And it's just such a shame

About the age in my bones

Along with the pain

About the youth and their sanity

How everyone's insane

No one has morals

They don't use their brain

Our future is cursed

When no compass remains

We're all running loose

Nobody's been trained

As I'm sipping my tea

Viewing failures in frames

12. Eyelash

A sudden sharp pain blinds me instantly

The pain is unbearable & I can barely see

Well, I can actually see but only from 1 eye

I'm okay, after a few tears

And it was only a single eyelash

IT.

WAS.

ONLY.

AN.

EYELASH.

13. Beautiful Little Stranger

Early morning hustle

Running in the rain

Trying to catch the late bus

Trying to keep it sane

Dripping from the weather

In a moving crowd

Trying not to stumble

Or express myself out loud

With every stop, it's getting tighter

My eyes are screaming DANGER!

Then she locks & smiles at me

What a beautiful little stranger

14. Not Disappeared

A fault within your system

I've become a glitch

I've gone far beyond

The invisible can't be fixed

Nowhere near your spectrum

Feeling like a spec

Floating off to nowhereness

To the land of the rejects

Searching for myself

Didn't realize I was lost

Wasted for your gain

Priceless was the cost

Placed upon the back burner

Burning in my fumes

Disregard my feelings

As long as you're in tune

As long as you come 1st

The world can sit and wait

Feeding you my fruits

While there's nothing on my plate

To someone, somebody is no one

But I'm someone to me

I'm still here, not disappeared

I can still see me

15. Better Than I

Everything I can do

You can do better

Everything I have taught

You can learn greater

Every step I have taken

You can take further

Every error I have made

You can make shorter

Every smile I have smiled

You can laugh louder

Every song I have sung

You can sing prouder

For every dream I have dreamt

You can make real

For every moment that was taken

You can now steal

For every step mistaken

I have cleared the path

For every problem I've tackled

I have solved the math

For every hurt that will come

I can't ease the pain

I taught you how to manage

And how to clean the stains

Climbing mountains

Fulfilling dreams

Raised you I did

To go further than me

Shining brighter

Than the brightest star

Better than I

Is what you are

16. I Can't Quit You

My beautiful monster

My stress reliever

My perfect storm

My backbone believer

I can't let go

I just can't quit you

When my mind is made

I start to miss you

With all honesty

My truth teller

Never steer me wrong

My love speller

Bumping heads

With every debate

I open the door

You close the gate

From 1 thru 10

The rate is eight

I won't stumble

You keep me straight

With different dishes

You stay on my plate

I just can't quit you

The time's too late

17. Eddison

You are my moon & stars
And all that's pretty in the sky
Looking out my window
In the silence of my nights

You are the autumn foliage
The slowly dancing leaves
Full of many colors
Effortlessly, dancing there for me

You are the hot summer sun
Beaming with such intensity
To not be confused
With anything less than sincerity

You are my beauty rainbow
After a rainfall

You are a brand new day
You are small & 10 feet tall

You are a winter storm
That decorates my window
Like a bag of marshmallows
The sweetest, softest snow

You are my solar system
Undeniably, including Pluto
No matter what's the distance
You know, I know, you know

18. I Don't Fear You No More

I don't feel it no more

Your slaps, your abuse

All the words you used

To try to break me in two

The brain games you played

The physical pain

The scare of your stare

Me hiding my shame

The constant apologies

Kept me by your side

The fear of me living

When I thought I would die

I admit at one point

They brought me down

The feeling was worthless
Felt less than a noun

The thoughts, I deserve this
In the back of my mind
In my ears like a drummer
It pounded me blind

I couldn't see what you saw
All the wrong inside me
When I am an ocean
You couldn't swim in my sea

I don't feel it no more
Your words are all empty
They once filled me down
Now I see they were envy

The weak one was you

You had no power

My talent was terror

As tall as a tower

I jumped off that ship

I swam to shore

I rather have drowned

Then to stay on aboard

You drowned in my world

You couldn't keep up the pace

The way to catch up

Was to spit in my face

To belittle my worth

I never came first

I was your blessing

While you were my curse

I don't see it no more

I've sharpened my sword

You may have won the battles

But, I won the war

19. Selfish Me

Loving you came easy

When all you wanted

Was to love me

You had very little expectancies

When all you wanted

Was to see me happy

Loving me was a challenge

When all I wanted

Was to love me

Never satisfied, very selfishly

When all I wanted

Was to see me happy

I'm sorry

20. Fuck Cancer!

Tattooed on my flesh

"Fuck Cancer"

You came quick

But I am faster

You can't slow me down

Or dim my shine

Just call me sunny

Stare and go blind

Back for round two!

Did you forget I'm a fighter?

Spinning my web

I'll tangle like a spider

Like a warrior in battle

I'll shed blood for mine

48

I know the odds

The scars you've left behind

But I don't stand alone

I stand protected

With the support of my angels

I stand connected

So Fuck You Cancer!

This battle, you will not win

With my prayers & protector

I proudly stand with him

21. I Lose Myself

Looking into the ocean of your eyes

I drown in you

The waves come crashing

I sink in you

I lose myself

Inside of you

Below sea level

In those big blues

Awakening

Like a morning brew

Healthy to my soul

Like *Abuela's stew

In a fairytale

Fascinated by you

Every page I turn

Think, this can't be true

Over the cuckoo's nest

I thought he flew

Like Nurse Hatchet

Cruel & rude

Then came you

With those ocean blues

The waves came crashing

And I drown for you

Abuela, Spanish word for Grandma

22. Father Time's Crime

Your pictures are fading

One flick at a time

They're slowly escaping

Father time's crime

Every day is a mystery

Do you know who I am?

Confused by my image

I'm your #1 fan

For you I am present

But I'm lost without you

You are slowly leaving

I don't know what to do

I walk in support

With my purple ribbon

But nothing is changing

You stay in your prison

Mommy it's me!

Do you know who I am?

Do you remember my name?

Do you understand?

Your pictures are fading

One flick at a time

They are slowly escaping

Father time's crime

23. I Know Who I Be

I know who I are

I know who I be

I may not speak proper

But you'll know what I mean

The accent is heavy

My culture is loud

I talk with a slang

My attitude is proud

I know where I come from

I know who I am

I know who is fake

I know who's my fam

Don't let me fool you

My grammar is good

I speak like my people

Home grown from the hood

So just take it easy

Come at me slow

With love & respect

Or I will lose control

I am what I eat

So don't feed me shit

I will come correct

If you come legit

24. 1ˢᵗ Choice

I only wanted to be your valentine

Through good & bad times

I wanted to be your 1ˢᵗ choice

Not what's next in line

I wanted you to bring me flowers

Maybe a chocolate heart

I wanted you to write me a letter

A few lines that would start a spark

I wanted you to notice me

In a crowded room

To smell my scent & just wonder

Where did she find that perfume?

I wanted you to follow me

Using just your stare

Ask around, inquire within

Who is that goddess there?

I wanted you to want me back

To be your valentine

I wanted you to choose me 1st

Not what's next in line

25. Until

I never thought you were the one for me

Until…

You were the one for me

26. Toothpaste the Burn

What's done is done

It can't be changed

It can't be twisted

Or rearranged

We can't go back

Reverse time

Unspeak the spoken

Rewrite the lines

Emotions exploded

Feelings hurt

Relationships damaged

Dragged in dirt

Tomatoes thrown

Booed off stage

The mic was dropped

A balled up page

Close your book

Lesson learned

Can't trust the world

Toothpaste the burn

What's done is done

It's not all fun

Dust off the dirt

Time to move on

27. The Blame Game

Chitty chitty bang bang

A repetitious game

It's dimming down the spotlight

Fizzing fuming flames

Like a Ferris wheel

Going round & round

Like a silent movie

Defining is the sound

Everything is the same

Everything has changed

Cutting simple corners

Everything is estranged

Playing the blame game

We're all pointing fingers

Fighting for the mic

When no one is a singer

Trying to be loudest

With our vocal skills

Nobody is being heard

Nobody is sitting still

Dancing with our demons

Right hand on the bible

A repetitious game

Everyone is a liar

28. Silent Teens

I grew her in me

Fed her full

Felt her movements

Some were cruel

It was all a blessing

No regrets

Upon her arrival

Laid her on my chest

Love at 1st sight

More like 1st feel

Time traveled quickly

With every meal

Cherished memories

Heart felt tears

Celebrating life

Same day each year

Fast forward time

I can't catch up

The silence kills me

I can't shut up

Sweet sixteen

Where did time go?

Who are you child?

I do not know

In my face

So far away

Want to squeeze you

In my embrace

Take your time

What's the rush?

In my face

Miss you so much

29. Make-up Master

Swollen eyes

Bloody lips

Hurtful words

Bruised up hips

Concealed up

Make-up master

Forget the past

Heal up faster

With every word

Apologies

Forgiveness counts

If you believe

Walking on eggshells

Must tiptoe

One wrong move

He will explode

"It's all my fault"

She believes her lies

She tells herself

Helps her survive

Respectful man

Professional field

Must save face

Hide the real

30. Position Erased

My mind is not sober

Distorted with pride

Admit to my wrongs

For so long I've denied

Chasing the uncatchable

I can never catch up

Three steps behind

Intentions corrupt

Fighting emotions

A few I made up

With the ticking of time

They turn to disgust

I promise, I promise

To myself it's a must

I suck in my tears

When my eyes want to bust

I'm running this race

I'm dying of thirst

Confused to the fact

Why I'm last and not first

I was number one

Now I don't hold a place

My mind is not sober

My position erased

31. Broken Chains

I didn't have much

I knew very little

Never really showed it

I was so brittle

A baby of a girl

A child with a child

Afraid of the future

The fashion, the style

Determined to make it

And raise a great man

I asked nothing from no one

With my mental plan

The struggle, a struggle

But I always won

Very well worth it

When I look at my son

A beautiful boy

A talented man

With his education

With his future plans

The past will not follow

He has broken the chains

With support by his side

He navigates the plane

32. Train Wreck

I am a mess

A total train wreck

With every plan

There is a rain check

Can't count on me

I don't follow thru

Social anxiety

With no social cues

Isolation

Is the name of the game

Deprivation

I play it in shame

I am a wreck

Not by design

So many emotions

Intertwine

I cannot breathe

I must confess

With every step

I am breathless

I'm a social butterfly

Somewhere inside

With every encounter

I run and hide

Hide and seek

In a pretty dress

Facial expressions

Cover up the mess

It's who I am

My one success

A pretty package

Stuffed and compressed

33. Beauty Boss Bitch

I put you on a pedestal

That's where you belong

Intelligent, reliable & independent

Because Mamma raised you strong

Throughout your many travels

Everything you've seen

It never tainted your views

In your future or beliefs

My little beauty boss bitch

Always taking charge

Don't like the path you're taking

You stop & disembark

You're beyond your years

See everything so clear

When it's time to keep it moving
You wipe away your tears

I put you on a pedestal
You will not settle for any less
When life gives you bullshit
You challenge every test

You know the path you're taking
No talk can make the switch
I put you on a pedestal
My little beauty boss bitch

34. Ghost

In a world full with billions

How can I stand alone?

In a house full of flesh

In a house that's not a home

In a farm full of feces

Everything smells like shit

Everyone is cheering

Wishing I would quit

Standing with a brace

Just for the support

Knowing when to fight

And what missions to abort

Knowing who are friends

And the fakeness of the fans

Trying to understand

The unplanned cannot be planned

In a world full of flesh

Everyone's a ghost

Learning what comes next

Comes from the next post

Everything smells like shit

What no one will admit

But if you wear the fashion

I guess the shoe must fit

35. Pablo

And I'm going crazy
But I'm not losing my mind
My thoughts are perfectly sane
My words, a bit unkind

And I'm high and I'm low
And I spit when I blow
And I verbalize my thoughts
And they're out of control

I speak 1st and think later
I'm a God and I'm greater
I'm an innovator and creator
Manic motions exaggerator

Like a child let me explain
What's going on in my brain

When my words are rapidly running

And I need a minute to refrain

Please don't kill the messenger

We are all media prisoners

If we're all talkers, where are the listeners?

It's been clearly stated, we are all visitors

No one seems to understand

I am thinking ahead of plan

I'm a movement not just a man

My name is a legendary brand

36. Father's Map

I tried to find myself

Following your tracks

Blue lines & red dots

In a folded up map

Following the road

You laid for my path

Doing the math

Studying the graphs

Trying to stay centered

To make you proud

Cutting my wings

So I can stay on the ground

To be who I wanted

When I wanted to fly

My wants were "far-fetched"

The stretch was "too high"

In finding myself

I found out the truth

I was only worth it

IF, I walked in your shoes

IF, I lived out your dreams

IF, I forgot all of mine

IF, I let you lead

While I stayed behind

To make you proud

I had to be YOU

Lose all myself

Be falsely untrue

I'm trying to find me

Following my tracks

Blue lines & red dots

In my folded up map

37. I Think I Can

I am in nowhere land

With the emotions of nothingness

With nowhere to go

Feeling frustrated from the emptiness

I must be full of helium

I'm floating away

And I'm okay with it

Because I don't want to stay

I must be somewhere

In a wishing well

With so much dripping

Everything is dark as hell

This place seems familiar

I've been here before

In the land of the losers

Where we're all at war

Searching for someone

Anyone for the pull

I see everyone staring

Ignore are the rules

Look away, invisible me

Avoid eye contact so you won't see

Then play the fool with apologies

"I didn't know, I'm so sorry"

I'm in nowhere land

Alone I stand

With so many fans

I think I can, I think I can

I always do, I always pull through

I stand alone, invisible you

You show up at my best

Pop quiz time, you failed the test

38. Secretly Sorry

What happened to me?

What happened to you?

With all of our promises

Our truth & "I do's"

We stayed here on pause

With all of our flaws

Secretly sorry

Holding our short straws

With no complaints

We thought it okay

With both of us drowning

No one to save the day

What happened to me?

I was quick with the speech

Expressing my wants

My thoughts & my needs

What happened to you?

So strong & obtuse

So brave with the truth

So rough & so smooth

Nobody knows

Where did we go?

We never quite left

We never did grow

39. Find a Feather

Words can be a beautiful thing

Combined with emotions

They can change a lonely world

Or be brutally explosive

When feelings find a feather

When a canvas finds its brush

When music find its rhythm

When a high releases its rush

Ink to paper, letters to words

Adjectives, nouns, throw in some verbs

Complete a sentence, a story told

The sound of music, chirping of birds

Like a ticking time bomb

The countdown will begin

3, 2, 1 release the rockets

Then we start again

40. Complete With Me

I am free

I choose to be

Whole in one

Complete with me

Don't feel bad

I'm not sorry

I come & go

No apologies

I enjoy your fun

Your company

But I enjoy the times

When it's just me

I am full

No emptiness

Relationship stress

My own address

I love me

Is that hard to believe?

I don't need

What you receive

I am free

Complete with me

All I need

Is the air I breathe

41. Sugar Beast

I'm unwinding

Eyelids closed

Scent so sweet

Like a rose

I'm floating off

My thoughts are none

I'm far away

I'm on the run

I feel the spinning

In the eye of the tornado

Everything is exactly

Where it should go

I feel the movement

Of the potion

Everything in sight

In slow motion

I am here

I'm in the air

I am there

I'm everywhere

My eyes wide open

I'm well alert

I can feel every bone

The pain of hurt

Cotton candy

Brings me peace

Stops the pain

The sugar beast

Helps me unwind

Helps me release

Willy Wonka

My sweetest feast

The clouds below

I'm floating off

Everything around me

Feels so soft

The hurt is slow

Almost gone

Sugar rush

Almost fun

Eyelids closed

I'm well aware

Feel no pain

But beware

The sugar beast

Can creep up

Fear the fun

You will erupt

42. I Play the Part

Don't let me fool you

I am not me

I am only the person

I allow you to see

There's so much more

Then meets the eye

I don't wear one

I wear many disguises

My costumes change

Constantly

I'm who you want

Halloween

A pretty face

With the coldest heart

You name the role

I play the part

I am honest

I am fake

Your sweetest dream

Your biggest mistake

Don't let me fool you

You fool yourself

On the pedestal

On the highest shelf

My make-up changes

You name the game

It's what you want

It's your picture frame

You let you fool you

I am just me

Playing the part

You want me to be

43. You! You! You!

No more words

Are left to be said

No more poems

Left to be read

No more tears

Left to be shed

No more plans

For our future ahead

You painted a picture

I held the brush

I laid the strokes

A painter's touch

You spoke the words

The colors would dance

So many promises

Full of romance

You, you, you

It was always you

When things fell apart

I was the glue

When you couldn't see

I showed you the view

When you couldn't walk

I wore your shoes

You seem to forget

Who held you down

When you had no one

Who was around?

Who was the one

That made you hear sounds

When negativity attacked

When you couldn't be found?

I found the peace

Within your soul

When you were alone

With no self-control

I found the pieces

That made you whole

That you always held

But too afraid to show

You, you, you

It was never me

To take the leap

And follow my dreams

To think of myself

And live selfishly

You! You! You!

It was never me

44. December 11th

I can't stop these eyes from leaking

On the worst day of my year

My heart floods me with memories

My face drowns from the tears

I know it's wrong of me

To play, rewind, replay

When you were so much more

Then the day you went away

But the hurt just keeps on coming

And I can't make it freeze

So please forgive me while they leak

Just forgive me please

45. Perfect Picture

Pretty picture painted perfectly

Put upon the pantry shelf

Pretty lady sitting silently

Sorrily, has no worth for self

Singing softly sad slow songs

With every step she takes

Reminiscing all her moves

Choices full of mistakes

Clipping coupons crazily

But never saves a cent

Stretching smile goes for miles

Still always seems so spent

Dripping diamonds dangling

A girl's one true best friend

"Look at me, he must love me"
Her damaging defense

Chasing Charming's shiny shoes
Never side by side
Material things by the load
Such a lonely bride

Look & listen lovely lady
This can't be your way out
Singing softly sad slow songs
While your cup is full of doubts

46. Who I Am

I'm twisting my brain

Trying to find the right words

To express my emotions

In a logical term

To come across basic

Is not my intention

So I'm rated below average

Must create with invention

Erase all I know

Mature all my lines

Think like a grown up

Bye-bye junior high

Develop my vocab

Change who I am

Design a new package

When I am my brand

Decisions undecided

I'm twisting my mind

When I'm loving my style

It is me it defines

A judgement was made

I'm pounding my gavel

Accept me for me

Or don't travel my travels

47. The Painting of the Proud

I suffer in my silence

My pain is my strength

When I'm on my knees

Is when I feel a wreck

When I cannot deal

With all that I feel

When I cannot hide

The torture is real

The image it's perfect

No one really knows

The power to uphold

And not lose control

I suffer in my silence

It's deafening to my ears

When everything's so loud

And no one else can hear

Invisible to the blind

With vision they can't see

I'm jumping off of my pages

Can anyone see me!?

I'm weak within my wreck

The quiet speaks loud

The image of perfection

The painting of the proud

48. Time

Time goes by

The clock don't stop

With every tick

There is a tock

With every blow

There is a pop

With every zap

There is a shock

Time goes by

Speed & fast

With no time

To make it last

Memories rushed

They can't be grasped

Emotions washed

Gone in a flash

Time goes by

It won't slow down

Rough with edges

Not smooth or round

It comes in loud

With silent sound

It gives you smiles

Along with frowns

Time goes by

Take your time

Don't let the rush

Steal your shine

Make it last

Wine & dine

Step by step

You'll be just fine

49. Not So Brave

Poison pistol

Not today

Go that direction

Not my way

Gossip gangster

Thugged out tongue

Words out loud

Can't be unrung

Slithering snake

Stay anonymous

Behind a screen

Stay venomous

Words of wisdom

Keep to yourself

Keep your opinion

Elf on the shelf

Not so brave

With your loose lips

Get confronted

Flip the script

With so much noise

Can't be found

Telephone tough guy

Never around

50. Pretty Princess

Pretty princess

Know your worth

Voluptuous body

It's not a curse

You are original

One of a kind

You are not your body

You are your mind

Be brave & strong

You are your strength

Never bow down

Be confident

Speak your peace

With respect

Choose your words

Be direct

You are a temple

And should be worshipped

Control your narrative

Write your manuscript

Pretty princess

Take control

Unleash your power

Fulfill your goals

51. Changes

I continue to struggle with my words

I continue to struggle with my movements

I struggle & struggle & struggle & struggle

But I have nothing to show, no improvement

I continue to walk on bare feet

When I have a perfectly pair of new boots

I chew on this bark, with flavor of less

When my trees, from them hang fresh fruits

I continue to write with this ink

I continue to wait for the slip

To come in the mail, handed to me

When a text would take just a blink

I continue, continue this journey

Living with times of the past

Taking my time when the world is so fast

Nowadays we all live in a flash

52. Who's to Say What to Say?

Who's to say what to say?

Trying to scar, clear the decay

Words of weapons in the air

In a fearless battle no one cares

Why do I do the things I do?

Rage runs rapid, the color cruel

Can't slow down, I have no breaks

When the blur is gone, my heart aches

I've spoken too much, the volume loud

Blows below belt, I am not proud

Truth was told not sugar coated

Notes were taken, fully noted

Regretful tones, came out so smooth

Secrets spilled from a kissing booth

Exposed to all just for shame

Who's to say what to say?

53. Karma

You trusted me

Shame on you

You betrayed me

Now I wear your shoes

You believed in me

Give me my applause

Taste your talent

Because, because

I ran from you

You chased your bait

You owed me one

It was time to pay

I charged you double

I'm one ahead

I took the lead

Led & misled

I played make believe

I learned from you

The game you taught

Was played on you

Next time think twice

With your deck of cards

When playing with hearts

Do not discard

54. Fighter

I'm running the race

But somethings gone wrong

I'm seeing the sun

But hearing sad songs

I'm moving my feet

I'm weary and weak

I get on my knees

My soul starts to speak

"I'm not ready to go

I'm trying to hold on

Lord, I know you can see me

Please make my strength strong"

My littles are little

They need mama bear

I'm begging for laughter

On my knees, in my prayers

I'm running this race

As fast as I can

I'm full speed ahead

To win is the plan

I wear my white ribbon

Because I am a survivor

With the sun on my face

I march on with the fighters

55. Tweety Bird

Sweetest secrets

To be held

I don't care

What they tell

Broken promises

No surprise

Never honest

Half were lies

Keep my past

In a vault

My high walls

Are not my fault

Truth be told

Not from me

A friend of mine

It's not honesty

Who said what?

Tweety birds

I said nothing

Fuck what you heard

I'm the mouth

In which to believe

It's all false

If it's not from me

I sing high

I sing low

I sing songs

I want you to know

Rock the Bells

Never tell

What you buy

Is what I sell

56. Fragile

I'm reaching out my arms to you

I'm screaming in this storm

I'm begging you to reach for me

My emotions are ignored

With silly smiles & loud laughs

Is how I hide my pain

With ups & downs I play the clown

So no one can see my shame

Another trip to patch it up

The concoction is your fix

It's your potion, I drink it up

Temporary is the mix

The same ole story, like a rerun

With time it never fails

I close my eyes, don't want to see

Suddenly I can read Braille

Broken glass, shattered hearts

To the fragile is not fair

I don't recall when it started

But the rain drops are now hail

I'm screaming in this storm

I'm begging for your reach

I'm drowning in emotions

And I'm speechless in my speech

The time is telling me to go

The light ahead is dim

My heart is tugging, just hold on

When all your love's for him

But I can't see ahead

And I'm scared to hit reverse

It's all the same & nothing's changed

And I am last when I was first

57. I Am Popping

Call me Orville Redenbacher

Because baby I am popping

Everything about me it's going

And baby I ain't stopping

I'm a tasty treat

I am butter & I'm cheddar

There's no reason to compete

I am better than the betters

I stand tall, I praise me

I don't need no other blessings

I'll be waiting here forever

Waiting for acceptance

So you can call me Colonel

I'm finger licking good

And if I fail, that's just success

A woodchuck chucking wood

There is no other option

Feel free to pity me

It fuels the fire in my soul

It pushes me to succeed

I'm but a simple kernel

Unlike the other corns

With the beauty of a rose

With the sharpest thorns

58. Tornado in a Box

I'm falling apart

Looking whole

With a pep in my step

And a facial glow

Show no signs

Poker face

Hidden talent

Lipstick & lace

Always helping

Can't help myself

Tornado in a box

On the closet shelf

Loudest laughter

Catching cramps

Cover the real

No time to revamp

Suffer the pain

No one to blame

Trying to maintain

A lifelong game

Pep in my step

Skip to my Lou

I'm just great

How about you?

59. Miss Regretful

I'm not ready to let go

I refuse to believe it's true

So when you tell me it's over

I refuse to believe we're through

I want to apologize

For all the pain I brought

I take it all back

Because it's all my fault

All the words of attack

All the scars then the salt

When I walked away

When you wanted to talk

You have grown so cold

The temperature it's freezing

I can barely see it

Our future it's leaving

Now I can't be found

I have lost my way

I'm living in a nightmare

Wake me up and please stay

Make it not be true

I take the nasty back

I didn't mean the mean

It was all an act

Tell me its okay

I want to erase the past

Start anew today

Remove my monster mask

Hello, how are you doing?

I don't think we've met

My name is Miss Regretful

Stay awhile with no regrets

60. A Mothers Concern

The constant concern

Never goes away

Not knowing the thoughts

Which stays & which strays

What is your next move?

Do you remember my words?

When I speak from the heart

Do they fly with the birds?

The fear you've gone deaf

It's louder than thunder

And I sit and I wonder

I starve from this hunger

New events with each chapter

In your book full of lines

So many pieces to your puzzle

They scramble my eyes

It's hard to see straight

What's true, what's a lie?

Your tone says you're crying

Your eyes, they stay dry

From mistakes you will learn

And the fire will burn

And I will still remain

With my constant concerns

61. I Run My Race

I run my own race

I am in no rush

I take my time

In life, there is so much

I compete with no one

Other than myself

Chances are a dime a dozen

And I'm always on my twelfth

We all make our mistakes

There's always another chance

I take the lead, roam the room

Pick & choose with whom I dance

There's 24 hours to a day

I never say "it's too late"

I mold my model with my clay
I disassemble & recreate

I compete with me
With the me of yesterday
Today I pray for tomorrow
I stay at bay & never stray

I take my time
I run my race
I don't look back
I don't play chase

62. What If?

Afraid of the future

Of the stars, of the high

The darkness, the beauty

The specs in the sky

The breeze in the air

The flow of my hair

Private thoughts we share

The labels we wear

Nothing's forever

I'm afraid of the loss

When your physical is here

I'm afraid of the frost

When the temperature drops

And with two there's a crowd

When no one is speaking

When the thunder's too loud

I'm afraid of the mirror

The person I see

With the magic of makeup

That person is not me

I'm afraid of the what if's

That hasn't occurred

The music of chirping

To take flight like a bird

63. Joyful Mess

Wiggle wiggle

Jiggle jiggle

With every dimple

Came a giggle

Full of laughter

Happiness

Unperfected

Joyful mess

1st to dance

With every beat

All eyes on me

Sitting in their seats

Wiggle jiggle

Wrinkles wrinkles

With every line

I share a dimple

Act my age

What does that mean?

Shut down the light

That beams in me?

I've earned my stripes

My leopard spots

I've swept the floors

And gave them a mop

I've walked the walk

I've crawled the miles

I've cried in silence

I've faked the smiles

I've paid my dues

My time has come

I'll eat my cake

Every piece, plus crumbs

64. Insecure Me

I've followed his lead

Right or wrong

Mostly misled

Still tagged along

Believed in his words

They were lyrically sung

Words of a magician

Magical tongue

The Wizard of Oz

Yellow brick road

A big block of clay

To perfectly mold

Tumbling down a hole

Just call me Alice

Trying to escape my world

With my thumping rabbit

A million miles a minute

Thinking a thousand thoughts

Doing what I was told

Living what I was taught

Insecure me

Full of insecurities

Searching for the answers

When they were all in me

65. Words of Attack

I'm sorry I hurt you
When I'm feeling attacked
I spit when I'm angry
I'm full of non-facts

My words are like daggers
They can hurt like hell
I know how to use them
Spread the funk of the smell

My talent is torture
It comes in sudden spurs
Introduction like lightning
Quickly gone, it's a blur

The tongue is long lasting
The scars never quite heal

Attached with emotions

Now frightened to feel

I'm sorry I hurt you

With words of attack

They spill out so easy

Yet hard to take back

66. Start Over

I loved you and lost you

Once before in the past

Until you realized it was greener

When you stood on your grass

Your return to me

Was no centerpiece

Everything was arranged

To have your needs pleased

I loved you and lost you

It's my turn to let go

Holding on to something

That refuses to grow

Emotionally numb

Is where I have gone

I want to start over
On somewhere else lawn

I want to pass the baton
I'm done with this race
Running in circles
In the same damn place

I love me, I've lost me
Living in your world
Following directions
Sinking in this swirl

Material overload
To keep me content
Emotionally empty
With the need to eject

I want to feel butterflies

I want to feel high

Adrenaline rush

I want to sky dive

I want to laugh out loud

I want to dance in a crowd

I want to showcase my talent

I want to stand solo and proud

I loved you and lost you

Once before in the past

It's my turn to sleep

And stand on my grass

67. Mission Aborted

All the promises promised

I take them all back

At the time they had meaning

When the trail had a track

Everything destroyed

Mission aborted

On bended knees

The message distorted

The cookie has crumbled

The fat lady sung

The cake you have eaten

Can't undo the tongue

I've been misled

The contract's been breached

A lesson been learned

The poison was bleach

The promises promised

A great song to sing

The steps must be taken

It's not just a ring

There's no turning back

Apologies not accepted

The position of second

Has been rejected

68. #1 Fan

You were my sister

Jackie & Roseanne

My ride or die

My right hand man

With different parents

From the same damn clan

Same grade & class

Kindergarten we began

Thru out the years

It was you and me, man

We had a mission

Shared the same dream plan

You got some talent

I'm your # 1 fan

High in demand

Blew up like the Big Bang

Now you're on stage

And you're doing your thang

You're in control

In total command

You took a tour

I took a tour with my fam

You took a turn

And forgot who I am

I laid back

Let you be the big grand

Proud of my sister

Who became the name brand

You living large

Left me back in La-la land

I watched you rise

While I sunk in quicksand

You are my sister

You grew high in demand

I understand

Still your # 1 fan

69. Loving Me

Color contacts

Lace front wigs

"Oh, no you didn't!?"

"Oh, yes I did!"

Feeling pretty

Judgement free

I like the image

My reflection sees

Floral dress

Some short, some long

Different moods

Can't go wrong

Gel tip nails

With designs

Sometimes with crystals

Always divine

Face contoured

Plumped up lips

Fake long lashes

Jiggle in my hips

I feel pretty

I'm so carefree

Let me be me

With my securities

70. Mi Gran Estrella

Mother of mine, mama mia

My best friend, mi mejor amiga

It's so weird how we've grown so close

We talk about everything, entre las dos

I can tell you my secrets

You won't tell a soul

You give me advice

Con razón

I look up to you

Because you are so strong

You have been my hero

For so very long

Mother of mine, my best friend

Madre mia, until the end

I've never thanked you for all you've done

Te doy las gracias, you're number one

You are my star, mi gran estrella

You are so beautiful, eres tan bella

Alone you raised us with respect

You taught us how to reach & stretch

You never left us

Always by our side

When the roads got rough

We all took the ride

Now I'm all grown up, y todavia esta

Para ti soy bebe y siempre sere

Con tu cariño me siento especial

Me sacas la sonrisas cuando me siento mal

My best friend you will always be

Te quiero tanto, I love you mommy

147

71. My Choice

I fell in love with her style

I fell in love with her voice

I fell in love with her talk

There was no choice

I fell in love with her heart

It allowed me to grow

I fell in love with her soul

Unfamiliar and unknown

It never mattered that she is a she

And I am a she

And she looks like me

Because we're loving life free

And in "WE" we believe

And it's okay, she's not a he

But, it matters to you

And I am confused

How the love others share

Can make others stare

Can make you so rude

The words you all use

Are violently cruel

When we're strangers to you

And I am confused

That it matters to YOU!

72. I Like Me Better

I like me better

Without the weekend drowning

Without the exposed navel

Without the one night crowning

I like me better

Without silly putty painting

With oversize T-shirts

When I obey all my cravings

I like me better

Without scary thoughts

Without thinking of my have nots

Without focusing on my faults

I like me better

When I'm honestly just me

When the fakeness fades

When I'm with my family

I like me better

73. Our Silk City

Home grown from the hood

Silk city to make it pretty

Once so prestige

Now decorated with pity

Home of the forgotten

Fetty put us on the map

Home of many stars

Our only glory isn't Wap

We had Lou Costello

Our great actor & comedian

Then our Salsa singer

Frankie Ruiz, Puerto Rican

How about our wide receiver

Let's give it up for Victor Cruz

With every touch down made

And his Salsa moves

The list goes on & on

These are just a few

A big shout out to our parks

And our Great Falls view

Let's hear it for our P-Town

Our poverty poor city

At one point so prestige

Our beautiful Silk City

74. Down For You

I remember I was down for you

Wore a crown for you

You were the King to this Queen

I would've drowned for you

I would've chased the moon for you

Changed the truth for you

Saw what you saw for you

Flip flopped on the world for you

Gave my all for you

Never lied to you

Still true to you

Stopped, dropped & rolled for you

I remember how you played with me

Mind games with me

Thinking what I saw

I didn't see, crazy

You wouldn't change for me

No cat & mouse chase for me

Never worked for me

Laid back, chillaxed, lazily

I was down, you see

Needed someone down for me

I believed in the bee

That stuck around sticking me

I couldn't see

It was all in me

The love of all loves

It was make believe

I was true to you

Because I'm true my dude

I wouldn't change who I am

Just to mimic you

75. Like The Northern Lights

Like a box of crayons

I have many shades

I have many motions

They alter with the change

The worst of them is gray

But mainly I feel blue

When it sneaks up on me

I don't know what to do

Like a ton of bricks

It crashes down on me

Paralyzed from the pain

All I want to do is sleep

With my eyes wide open

In a zombie state

My days become routine
My best is less than great

Then we have the green
I'm painted with jealousy
For those of you so brave
To follow all your dreams

Yellow it's for the shine
I feel deep down inside
And when it starts a shining
It's when I feel alive

I have many colors
I have breath taking sights
With my solar winds
Like the Northern lights

76. My Motivator

I am so unique

You're my motivator

With every word you speak

Imaginary line, equator

I bow down to no one

Like you bow down to me

You are such a worshipper

You praise me on your knees

With every step I take

There's something to be said

You always seem to walk behind

I walk three steps ahead

You think of me way to much

Vocalize, verbally

I'm on your lips, constantly

I drain you mentally

My Mr. Magic motivator

My Mr. Monster lie creator

My you can never be like me

My everything I do hater

I'm so high, I can't see you

When you're so far below

I shine bright, I'll always glow

My Mr. Monster invisible

77. You Are

You are

The beauty in a rose

Sung in a song

Written in a poem

Blown in the wind

From the warmth

Of the sun

Beaming on my face

On a breezy kind of day

With the scent

Of the ocean

With the crashing

Of the waves

You are to me

78. 100 Times

I don't want to hear it

Another apology

I've heard them 100 times

"Baby please, I'm sorry"

I can't do this anymore

While you're giving me a cheater

You can't teach a dog new tricks

You've made me a believer

You can't change who you are

You don't even try

You promised me a knight in armor

But you're a below basic guy

You're no better than the next

Actually you're worse

I will always love me more

I will always love me first

I don't want to hear it

Pack your bags and walk away

Take your tears and sorry "sorries"

And stay that way, away

79. Traditions

Remember back then

When we didn't have much?

Couldn't wait for the holidays

Excited from the rush

The school year's begun

Around the corner is Halloween

Inventions for costumes

We didn't have much money

No school on Thanksgiving

The whole family came over

No one thought they were better

Noses up or high shoulders

December starts the countdown

For the grandest one of all

The jolly one might stop over

No school, the whole week off

Do you remember our family?

How it began to slowly change

Now we barely keep in contact

Not even on the holidays

We don't share each other's secrets

We don't follow a tradition

Now holidays I spend it singing

A one-man band musician

80. Live

Feel free to fly

Free to feel

When you are hurt

Feel free to heal

Feel the joy

Feel free to smile

Laugh out loud

And stay awhile

Walk the plank

Take the leap

Swim the laps

Feel the heat

Live a little

Take the shots

Don't give up

Give it all you got

Give to others

It'll all come back

When you're in need

Karma will attack

Take from no one

If they can't spare

Feel free to wonder

And stay aware

81. Over Budget

Everything you're selling

I can't believe I'm buying

Money is flowing

From the sales of your lying

Pockets are empty

I now pay by crying

My soul is now leaving

You're killing me, I'm dying

Your words don't mean much

Now they're words just spoken

I've been easily replaced

My heart you have broken

I have no more to give

I'm feeling so small

When you were my world

And now I'm nothing at all

I don't understand why

When did you stop feeling?

I do believe now

I must start my healing

I must let you go

Release all this pain

I can't hold on to you

Deleting the frames

I've bought all I can

My budgets gone over

I can't buy more lies

When each day they grow colder

I can't keep on holding

When there is nothing to hold

I can't keep you warm

When you're making me cold

82. Drip Drip

You make my eyes roll back

When you go down down

You make my back arch

As your face drown drown

You make her sweat happy

With every lick, drip drip

Got me talking double

When your lips are on my lips

Questioning my sexuality

Because you're that great

Eating like a savage

Everything on your plate

Going back for seconds

You're so very greedy

Double like my stutter

Opposite of speedy

Trying to catch my breath

While my head is spinning

Talking talking double

I know, you know I'm winning

Dripping from your chin

Here comes the main event

Twisted like a pretzel

I'm cumming, gone & went

83. "Lovers Lane"

This road we travel, "Lovers lane"

A 2 way road that goes both ways

I can't do it all, meet me half way

To continue our journey, without the pain

My headlights dim, my gas it's low

The car oppose, your speed it's slow

I need a sign, something must show

So I can drive, so we can grow

Hit your gas, don't reverse

Let's move ahead, don't rehearse

It must be real, I must come first

When I'm thirsty come quench my thirst

I need to feel you feel the same

You need to show the words you say

You need to meet me at least half way

To continue our journey down "Lovers lane"

84. Limbo

When all is right

I go left

I feel a mess

When I can't impress

Myself, it's a struggle

I cannot fix

I'm drowning in air

The splash of mist

Sinking in steps

It's like quicksand

I can't find footing

In the outer land

If I'm not a groupie

I am a fan

Of myself

Without a plan

With no direction

Where do I go?

No path was laid

I lay in limbo

Floating off

Inside of me

Fake the funk

So no one can see

They are blind

It's not just me

I am free

Still trapped in me

When they are wrong

I give apologies

People pleaser

Unpleased to me

85. Ashamed

Walk away from it all

Easier said than done

When the addiction is strong

The drug? You're the one

Help can't help me

When I can't help myself

The image in the mirror

Even that's starting to melt

My strength is growing weaker

My weakness it's on strong

I don't know what is right

When everything seems wrong

He will never see me

Not even at my best

The feeling that he brings on

That feeling's name is less

The needle it's in my vein

The addiction shares your name

I'm high when you are near

When you're gone I feel ashamed

Every day I disappear

Just a little more

When the answer is in my face

And only I control the cure

86. My Music

You are the wind I need

That blows me

In the direction

Of inspiration

The red traffic light

That makes me think twice

The octagon stop sign

That keeps me in line

I see the future

With advice that's crucial

I take it to heart

Because the feeling is mutual

What's best for me

Is what's best for you

What's best for you

Is for us to continue

To weather the storms

Fight for this us

Misleading to others

Calmly we rush

You are the music

I dance to alone

That no one can hear

But I know that you know

87. I Stand Alone

I'm running on fumes

No gas in the tank

My time is on over

With no cash in the bank

Pockets are empty

Schedule is full

Doing for others

I'm such a damn fool

Where are my people

When I am in need?

Looking around

They're not here for me

The city's alive

Nobody sleeps

Everyone is yelling

Nobody speaks

I follow the crowd

What is the fuss?

There's no one to ask

There's no one to trust

I'm running on fumes

My pockets are empty

In a crowd I roll solo

In my hand, there's a venti

And I stand alone

Alone I run free

Like mama would say

No one will love me like me

I've run out of fingers

Counting my blessings

No gas in the tank

Stress less & still flexing

88. I Believe, I Believe

I believe in the thunder & the storms

I believe in the sadness in my soul

I believe in the invisible that is born

Blind to those who do not know

I believe in the joy that comes around

That slowly creeps, that's seldom found

I believe in the volume, the silent sounds

Max on 10 floating in the clouds

I believe what I see with my eyes

Words can't change or rearrange my sight

I believe in the power, the righteously right

I believe in the darkness I feel at night

Tiptoeing, I still hear the creeks

My eyes are closed, you kiss my cheek

Doing 60 hours makes you complete

Can you still hear when the silence speaks?

I believe loneliness should be left alone

Makes no sense in a crowded home

I believe in the emptiness in my soul

Don't call back my silent phone

I believe with distance we'll reunite

I might return if you take flight

I believe in the thunder, I believe in the light

I believe the darkness can shine as bright

89. Full Of Doubts

Situations change

Well, who knew?

Rearranged

Something new

Feeling strange

So confused

Who am I?

Who are you?

Sudden sadness

Lingers around

Where am I?

Can't be found

Dancing solo

Spinning around

Why is this silence

So damn loud?

Engines roaring

I'm on the go

Sitting still

Laying low

Physical state

Is just for show

Mentally sinking

Down below

I want to go

Where do I go?

You are she

The only home I know

Disappear

Get out of here

I don't drink

Pour me a beer

What was said?

Zoning out

Soul is thirsty

Spiritual drought

Words were lost

Please don't shout

I'm for sure

Full of doubts

Give me a minute

Invisible pain

Silently hurting

Feeling ashamed

Situations change

And I remain

Trying to catch up

And remind my brain

90. Follow the Rules

Talk to me softly

Turn down the lights

Come wet my lips

Travel the night

Let's take our time

Enjoy the view

I'll show you the way

As you follow the rules

Come walk with me

Show me your braille

Tell me your story

Make me exhale

Without using your words

Make me want more

With all due respect

Keep me onboard

Don't forget I'm a lady

Let's keep it classy

Let's keep it clean

Until I make it nasty

Come wet my lips

I'll show you the pace

Let's travel like turtles

Let's win this race

91. Tsunami

I can never grab you

To put you in my pocket

So I settle for this ornament

In a heart shaped golden locket

Something I can hold

When I'm screaming for your soul

In my silent secrets

When I know I'm not that bold

I could never place you

In my atmosphere

And like a wave, tsunami

You suddenly appear

Lucky for the moments

A sliver of your time

To place me in your universe

When you belong in mine

We're always lost in time

We can never get it right

We share the moon & stars

Different days with different sights

For just another moment

I want to put you in my pocket

Knowing you are safe with me

Before you blast off like a rocket

92. Feed the Beast

Don't try to fix me

I am not broken

Beyond repair

Shattered and outspoken

Don't try to save me

I am not drowning

Lacking emotions

Emotionally starving

Feed the beast

A sexual feast

That is in need

Of physical release

Calm the storm

This natural disaster

With millions of followers

In lack of a master

Warm the cold

Temperatures dropping

Hyperthermia is setting

The fish are flopping

I am not lost

I know where I stand

Don't try to find me

I'm first in command

93. We're All Different

I see no color

I see heart

I see we're different

What sets us apart

I have no fear

Of what they think

Poison words

In an ice cold drink

Gives me strength

Feed the fuel

Enrage the anger

Makes me the fool

We are different

Aren't we all?

Many shades

Short, medium, tall

Religion, race

Financial aid

Daddy's money

Brave & afraid

You are different

Does not mean better

26 alphabets

Must work together

To form a word

Complete a phrase

The night must come

To welcome the day

I see heart

We are not the same

So many potions

Isn't that great?

94. Tortured Souls

Tortured souls

Gathered as one

They wet their lips

Labeled as fun

Some to escape

Their privileged lives

Others to forget

Their kids and wives

To others it's a job

They work full-time

They gather to forget

To rewrite their lines

Blame the world

It's all their fault

Thoughts distorted

The thoughts they thought

Misunderstood

No one understands

Tortured souls

They form a clan

They wet their lips

Together they're one

Nothing in common

Except the rum

95. I Pray

I've been down

Emotionally low

Depression on high

From sorrows, a pro

I've been hungry

Didn't know where to go

Spiritually starving

Didn't know the unknown

I wanted to go

Run away from it all

Lost all my strength

To walk so I crawled

I never gave up

When I knew I was broken

I picked up the pieces

And spoke the unspoken

Words just poured out

I didn't know what to say

Words of confessions

Released me that day

Now at peace I pray

It calms my soul

Clears my view

Completes me whole